Drawing

Drawing

The Only Drawing Book You'll
Ever Need to Be the Artist
You've Always Wanted to Be

Kathryn Temple

LARK BOOKS

A Division of Sterling Publishing Co., Inc.
New York

Editor:
JOE RHATIGAN

Creative Director,
 Book & Cover Designer:
CELIA NARANJO

Photographer:
STEVE MANN

Editorial Assistance:
DELORES GOSNELL

Proofreader:
KAREN LEVY

Photo Credits

SSGRP.com:
pages 55 and 56

Kathryn Temple:
pages 30 and 32

Joe Rhatigan:
pages 55 and 56

Library of Congress Cataloging-in-Publication Data

Temple, Kathryn.
 Drawing / Kathryn Temple.
  p. cm. — (Art for kids)
 Includes index.
 ISBN 1-57990-587-0 (hardcover)
 1. Drawing—Technique—Juvenile literature. I. Title. II. Series.
NC655.T38 2005
741.2—dc22
                                    2004017909

10 9 8 7

Published by Lark Books, A Division of
Sterling Publishing Co., Inc.
387 Park Avenue South, New York, N.Y. 10016

© 2005, Kathryn Temple

Distributed in Canada by Sterling Publishing,
c/o Canadian Manda Group, 165 Dufferin Street
Toronto, Ontario, Canada M6K 3H6

Distributed in the United Kingdom by GMC Distribution Services,
Castle Place, 166 High Street, Lewes, East Sussex, England BN7 1XU

Distributed in Australia by Capricorn Link (Australia) Pty Ltd.,
P.O. Box 704, Windsor, NSW 2756 Australia

If you have questions or comments about this book, please contact:
Lark Books
67 Broadway
Asheville, NC 28801
(828) 253-0467

Manufactured in China

ISBN 13: 978-1-57990-587-3
ISBN 10: 1-57990-587-0

For information about custom editions, special sales, premium and corporate
purchases, please contact Sterling Special Sales Department at 800-805-5489
or specialsales@sterlingpub.com.

Contents

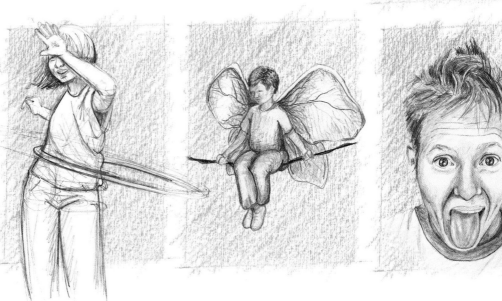

Foreword

I was lucky. When I was about six, my family met a spunky 76-year-old woman named Sylvia. She was the first real-live grown-up artist I had ever met. She could draw **anything**. She always took a long time looking at what she was drawing, and then she'd draw a little bit, and look up again. When she finished, it looked just like the thing or person she was looking at! One day, I asked her how she did it and she answered, "The most important thing an artist can do is pay attention. An artist needs to take the time to really look at and SEE what he or she is drawing." She went on to say that most grown-ups go through life without really noticing things. She said the other part was practice: she had been drawing for almost 70 years!

I spent many afternoons drawing and painting with Sylvia; she taught me real-live artist tricks, such as how to see (and draw) light and shadow and how to really capture the shape of something. This book contains all the important information that Sylvia taught me, as well as a bunch of other things I've picked up over the years as an artist. One of the things I've learned over time is that there are all kinds of secret lessons, techniques, and drawing tricks that artists understand. These tools will help make you the artist you've always wanted to be. You decide when, where, and how you use the different tools, but the more tools you have at your disposal, the more tricks you have up your sleeve, the greater your ability will be to express yourself and to create amazing pieces of artwork. Whether you're brand new to drawing or have been drawing forever, this book has something for you: it can help get you started or help you bring your drawings to the next level.

After many years, I finally figured out Sylvia's secret: all kids are artists. In fact, everyone starts out as an artist—it's just some people have most of the artist squeezed out of them by the time they grow up. Sylvia didn't treat me like a little kid when she was teaching me how to draw; she treated me like an artist—because I already was one, and so are you.

Everyone Can Draw

Some kids know they can draw as surely as they know they can eat. Others aren't confident they can draw a stick figure. No matter how you feel about your drawing, this book is for you.

The best way to use this book is to start at the beginning and work your way through it with your pencil and paper always ready for drawing and exploration. Each of the activities in these pages builds on the others. In other words, to draw the bodies in Chapter 7, you'll need to know how to draw the toilet paper tubes in Chapter 3. (Who knew you could draw bodies using toilet paper tubes!?)

Chapter 1 sets the stage for the rest of the book by showing you how to see the world the way an artist sees it.

Once you've gotten your creative mind wide awake, move on to line drawing in Chapter 2. Here you'll play around with finding the simple shapes in complicated objects.

Chapter 3 explores light and shadow, and your drawings will start jumping off the page!

Chapter 4 provides some fun tricks that help keep things in proportion as you transfer what you see in the world onto your drawing paper.

Explore the amazing techniques of perspective in Chapter 5. You won't believe how convincing your drawings will become—you'll feel as if you could walk right into them and take a stroll!

Chapters 6 and 7 take the mystery out of drawing people by breaking down faces and bodies into simple shapes you've already practiced drawing.

In Chapter 8 you'll take what you've learned and set yourself loose on the playground of your imagination.

Have fun and draw, draw, draw!

Drawing Rules to Live By or Life Rules to Draw By

1. There is no one right way to draw.

Don't believe me? Collect 100 amazing artists in a room and have them draw the same chair. What do you get? One hundred very different chair drawings. If you can get your brain around that, you'll have a lot more fun drawing and seeing the unique, strange, and amazing art that comes from you. **You're the only artist in the world who can draw the way you do.** Give yourself time to find and explore your personal drawing style.

2. Don't compare your artwork to other people's.

If you must compare your work to anything, compare it to your own. Notice how you have grown or improved as you practice. Pay attention to what you like most about your drawings.

3. There's really no messing up.

If you make a mark you're not crazy about, try to see it differently. Can you work it into the drawing? Let your drawing surprise you. It can take on a life of its own and help take you in directions you might not have gone if you hadn't been paying attention. Be surprised by your accidents, instead of beating yourself up over them.

4. Practice.

If you've never drawn before, start drawing. If you already draw, draw more. You have to be willing to make "bad" drawings in order to make good ones.

5. Don't stress out about showing your drawings to people.

As a matter of fact, you don't have to show your drawings to anyone if you don't want to. Do whatever you have to do to keep yourself from being overly concerned about the finished drawing.

The Drawing Toolbox

9B: makes very, very dark marks

6B: makes very dark marks

2B: softer than HB, makes dark marks

#2 or HB: a good middle-of-the-road pencil

2H hard lead: makes light marks

6H harder lead: makes really light marks

White pencil: for adding highlights on colored paper

All you need to draw is a pencil, some paper, and a sketchbook. If you want to experiment with different tools, check out these cool drawing supplies.

Why Pencil?

Pencils are great because you can just relax and draw without ever worrying about "messing up." They're erasable, smudgeable, and affordable. Most of the drawings in this book are done in pencil. Pencil lead (which is actually graphite) varies from very soft to very hard. The softest leads make the darkest marks. The harder leads leave much lighter marks, even if you press down very hard. Charcoal and pastels are sort of like pencil middles without the wood. They tend to be dusty and smudge easily.

Pastels

Charcoal

Paper

Papers vary in texture. You get very different effects depending on the combination of pencils and paper you use. Some papers have a very smooth surface. Others have more of a tooth (or texture). Rougher papers hold on to the pencil graphite better, especially with really dusty "pencils" such as charcoal and pastels.

Erasers

You can use the eraser at the end of your pencil if it has one. Otherwise, you can buy gum, rubber, or kneaded erasers. You don't rub a kneaded eraser over your paper. Instead, you press it into the area you want to erase and lift it off.

What About Pen?

I don't usually encourage artists to start off drawing with a pen. Why not? Well, you can't erase pen, and you can't shade your drawings by blending (see page 35). Having said that, pen drawing can be fun because it can create a more polished looking drawing. Also, since I encourage you not to erase too much, using a pen will keep you from erasing every little mistake you think you make. Finally, since you can't smear and blend pen, you can practice other shading techniques such as cross-hatching and stippling (see page 35 for more on these techniques).

Kneaded erasers

Gum eraser

Rubber erasers

11

Chapter One

Open Your Artist's Eyes

I have known quite a few young artists who start off being really worried about making things perfect. Before they start to draw, they'll reach for a ruler or ask for something round to trace in order to make a perfect circle. I tell them, "I've been drawing for more than 25 years, and I still can't draw a perfect circle or a perfectly straight line." Making a great drawing or being a fabulous artist isn't all about having a super-steady hand; it's about how you see, how you look at the world, and how you interpret the information that your eyes receive. This type of seeing goes beyond the regular seeing you're doing right now. It's like putting on a pair of magic glasses and suddenly noticing shadows, the way sunlight passes through a window, and lots of other things most people fail to notice.

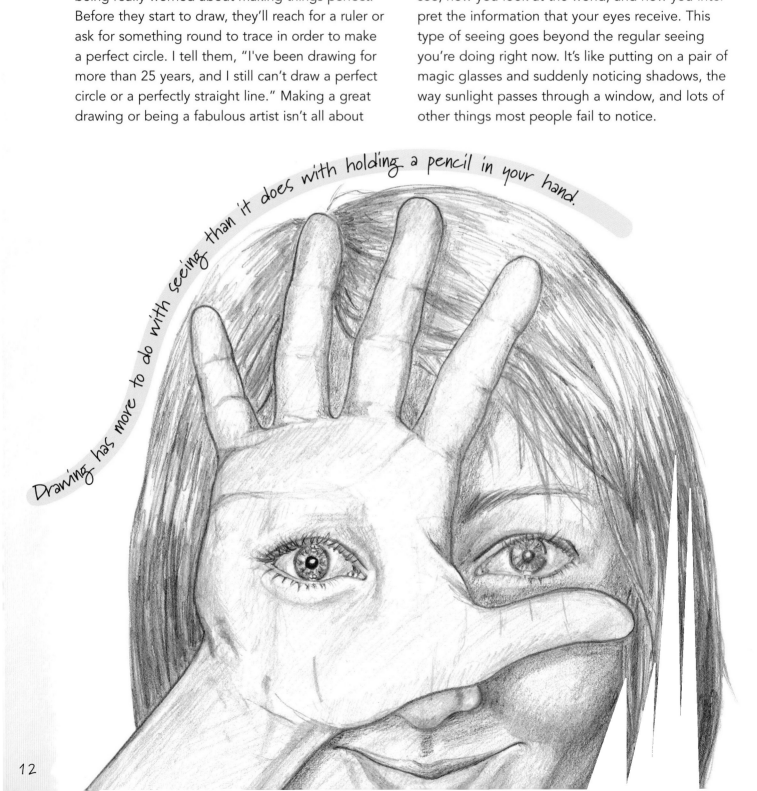

Drawing has more to do with seeing than it does with holding a pencil in your hand!

Different Types of Seeing

The brain is divided into two halves (or hemi-spheres) and each has different strengths and abilities. Our left brains are our centers for language, math, and symbols. Our right brains are our centers for imagination, association, and creativity.

Most of us grow up in worlds that teach us to use our left brain far more than our right brain. Imagine the problems one might have trying to do something creative, such as drawing, with the left side of her brain. Because we're so used to using our left brain all the time, this is often what happens. Our left brain can even get in the way of us actually seeing what we're looking at. It steps in and says, "Excuse me, but I have a nice easy little symbol here that will represent that thing you're trying to draw."

So, you end up with this

instead of this.

All it takes to overcome an underused right brain is practice and a little trickery.

So, keep reading!

Looks Can Be Deceiving

Here are three images that you'll identify pretty quickly. But, there is more than one way to see them! You might see them one way as you first look at them, but in order to see the second image hiding in these illustrations, your right brain is going to have to help you out.

What do you see here?
Do you see the back of a young woman's head? That's what most people see. Try to look at it differently. Can you also see an image of an old lady with a big nose?

What do you see here?
Do you see two faces looking at each other, or do you see a fancy drinking glass? Can you see both?

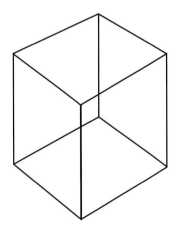

This is a normal cube, right?
Can you see the top of the cube, as if you're looking down at it? Or how about the bottom of the cube, as if it's floating above you and you're looking up at it? Can you see it both ways? If you're having trouble seeing what I'm talking about, take a look at the two cubes below that have one surface darkened.

These two cubes are drawn the exact same way as the first one, but the darkened surface gives you a visual clue about how to "see" the cube.

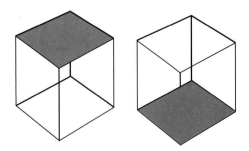

Scribble Art

Draw a continuous line on your paper. Don't pick up your pencil—just keep curving and swirling and switching directions until you have a tangle that travels over the whole page. Now, take some time to look at your tangled drawing. You'll see that where your line crosses, intersects, and overlaps itself, it made lots of different shapes you didn't mean to draw. Can you see anything that looks like something in real life?

At first, you may not see anything at all. That's probably your left brain trying to convince your right brain not to have any fun. But look at what I found in my drawing. Do you see how the shapes I found don't look exactly like a bird, a fish, or a cat mask? The shapes suggested those things to me. You might look at the same line drawing and find a bunch of entirely different things.

If you want, you can color in some of the shapes that you found in your drawing. Or you can keep your drawing purely abstract.

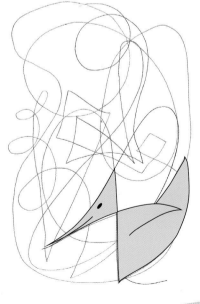

Look! A bird, a fish, and when turned upside down, a wild cat mask!

No Peeking!

A *contour drawing* is another name for a line drawing. A *blind contour drawing* is one where you don't look at your drawing as you draw it. Instead, you keep your eyes locked on the object you're drawing—you never look at your paper, and you don't lift your pencil from the paper the whole time. These are two blind contour drawings I made of a chair and a houseplant.

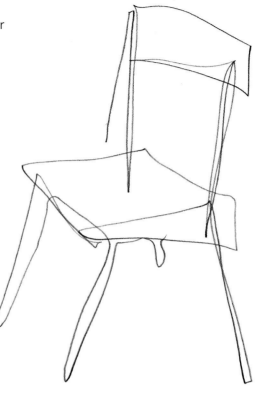

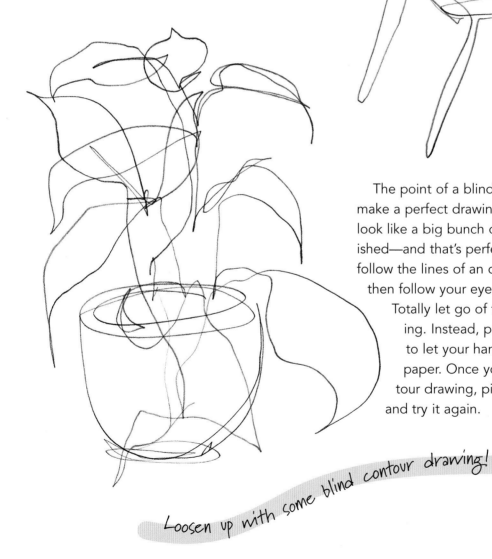

The point of a blind contour drawing isn't to make a perfect drawing. In fact, your drawing may look like a big bunch of scribbles when you're finished—and that's perfectly great. The point is to follow the lines of an object with your eyes and then follow your eyes with your pencil.

Totally let go of the outcome of your drawing. Instead, pay attention to how it feels to let your hand move freely across the paper. Once you've finished one blind contour drawing, pick something new to draw and try it again.

Loosen up with some blind contour drawing!

Upside Down Drawing

This is a great exercise for your right brain. When you turn something you recognize upside down, you can short-circuit the interference from your left brain. It makes it easier for you to resist the temptation to draw what you "think" you see—instead of everything your artist's eyes see.

Try drawing this picture as is. Resist the temptation to turn it right-side up.

Draw from upside-down magazine images.

Abstract Magic

Trace the four blank squares below onto a piece of paper. Next, draw (don't trace!) each of the four abstract designs on page 19 into one of the blank boxes on your paper. When you're drawing, think about where a line begins in relation to the corner of a box.

Try this technique with photographs or illustrations from magazines.

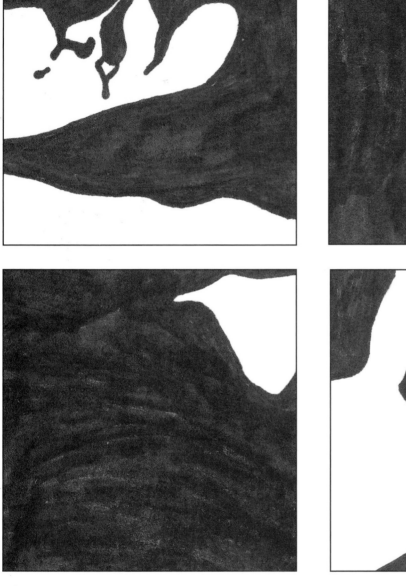

Now, cut out your four abstract drawings and see whether you can piece them together on the grid on page 18 to make a recognizable image. By dividing the image into four abstract-looking shapes, you are more likely to stay in your right-brain mode while you're drawing. Your left brain can't recognize the shapes as symbols for other things and interrupt the process. Turn to page 110 to see what you've drawn.

Practice all the previous activities whenever you feel like your left brain is getting in the way.

Chapter Two

Line Drawing

If you take a look around, you'll notice that there aren't a lot of actual lines in the world. That's because the world is made up of three-dimensional objects with shape and form. Lines, like paper, are flat. The lines we use in drawing often represent the edges of an object, or the point at which one thing overlaps or bumps up against another thing. Learning to draw with line is like learning a new language. You have to translate what you see—three-dimensional objects that take up real space—into the two-dimensional language of line.

The beauty of the language of line is that there aren't hundreds of thousands of new words to learn. As a matter of fact, there are really just four basic "elements of shape" that can be used to draw anything you see:

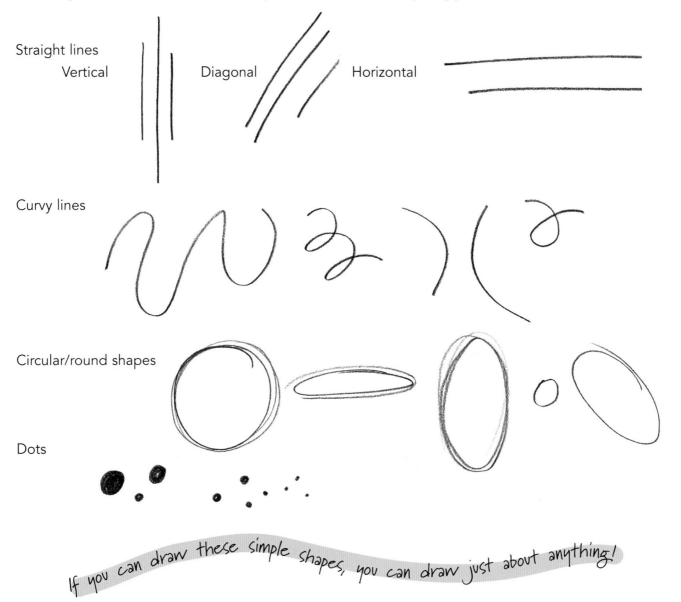

Straight lines
  Vertical   Diagonal   Horizontal

Curvy lines

Circular/round shapes

Dots

If you can draw these simple shapes, you can draw just about anything!

Draw Using Simple Shapes

Use the simple shapes in the left-hand column to draw the objects on the right.

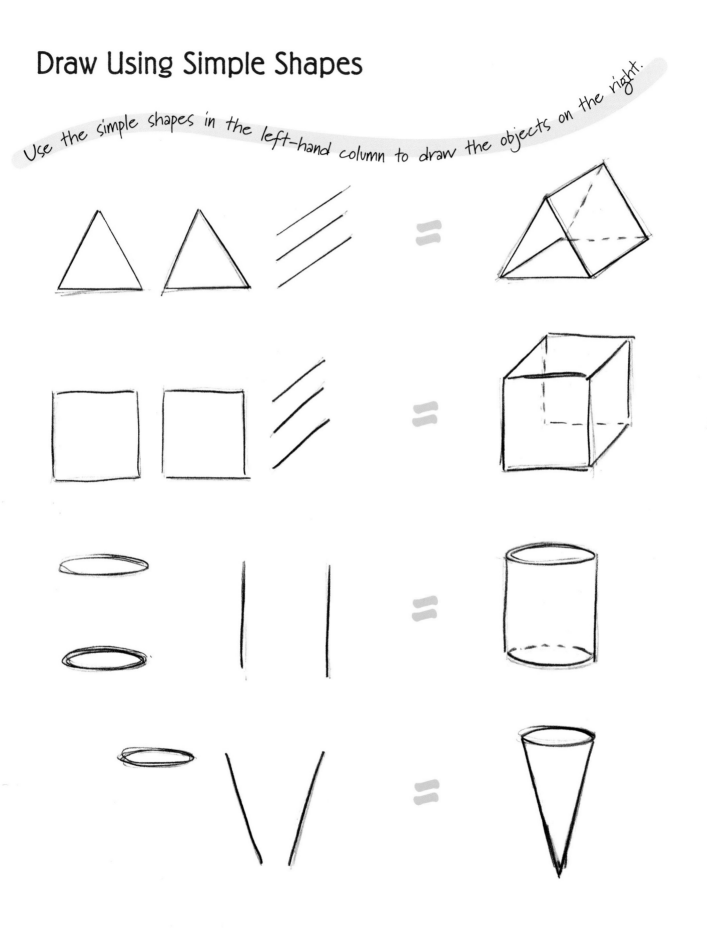

Simple shapes lead to marvelous things.

Build your fireplace with these simple shapes.

you can definitely draw this! Give it a try!

Just when you thought you'd be drawing cubes and flower-pots for the rest of your life, here's an example of what some simple shapes can produce.

Shapes All Around You

Now that you know the world is made up of simple shapes, the next part of line drawing is being able to recognize the simple shapes on page 20 in the objects you want to draw. So, instead of just seeing a cat, you're also seeing the circles, curves, and lines that give that cat its shape. Training your artist's eyes to find these simple shapes is the second part of learning the language of line, and this new language will help open up the world of drawing to you.

Study the objects around you. Really look at them. What basic shapes do you see in a car? How about a desk lamp? Your hand? With a little bit of play and practice, you'll learn to see the triangles in an open door, the circles in an apple, the curvy lines in the face of a cat.

Find these shapes in the photograph of the glass.

Check out all the triangles in this stack of books.

Turn to page 110 to see the shapes over the photographs.

Positive and Negative Space

As you practice identifying shapes in objects, you may notice another place to look for shapes in the world: in the space around and in between the things you're drawing. This is called *negative space*.

Take a look at these two doors. One is opened toward you and the other is opened away from you. Both door pictures have long, thin triangle shapes in them. In the first photograph, the triangle shapes can be found in the door itself, in the *positive space*. In the second photograph, the triangles mark the space above and below the open door; they mark the negative space.

If the door opens toward you, the triangle shapes will be above and below the door frame.

If the door opens away from you, the triangles will be on the inside of the door frame.

Drawing Positive and Negative Space

Find a door that you can sit directly in front of. Open it about a foot or so.

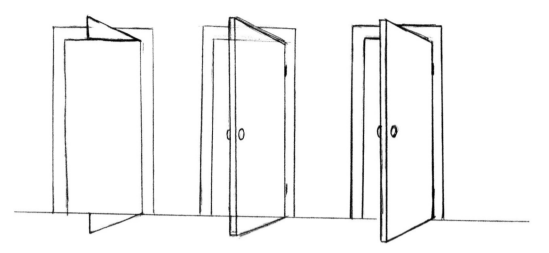

Draw a door that opens toward you.
1. Draw the door frame, and add your triangle shapes.
2. Draw the line for the edge of the door, and then turn that line into a long skinny rectangle so the door looks like it has some thickness.
3. Add hinges and a doorknob and erase the lines of the door frame that are behind the door.

Draw a door that opens away from you.
1. Draw the door frame, and add the negative-space triangles inside the frame.
2. Add the edge of the door.
3. Erase the shortest side of each triangle and add the doorknob and hinges.

Drawing Apples

Often, when people are asked to draw an apple, they draw the left-brain symbol for an apple: a circle with a little line for the stem. And while an apple does have a roundish shape, its form is more complex than a simple circle. It has many circles hiding beneath its skin!

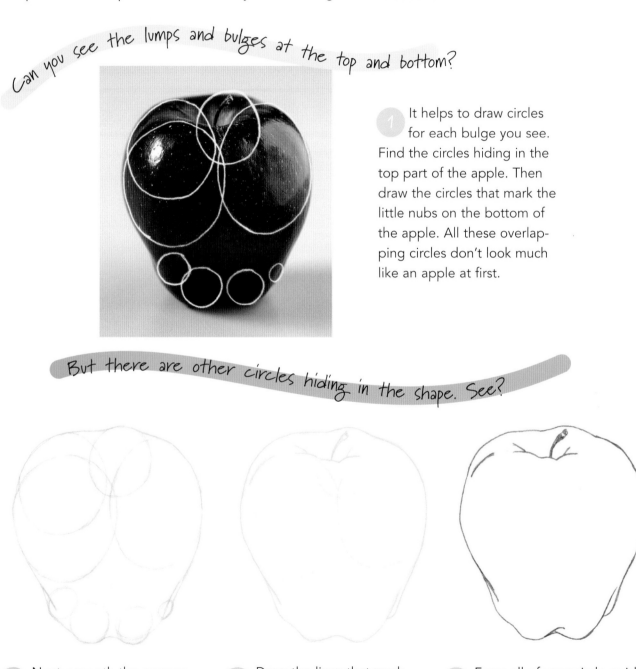

Can you see the lumps and bulges at the top and bottom?

1 It helps to draw circles for each bulge you see. Find the circles hiding in the top part of the apple. Then draw the circles that mark the little nubs on the bottom of the apple. All these overlapping circles don't look much like an apple at first.

But there are other circles hiding in the shape. See?

2 Next, smooth the connections between the circles by adding the skin of the apple.

3 Draw the lines that mark where the apple curves in toward the stem.

4 Erase all of your circle guidelines. Ta da! A lovely apple.

From Apples to Cats

Of course, cats are more complex forms than apples, but we approach drawing them the very same way. First, we identify the biggest, most basic shapes in their bodies. Then we identify lumps and bulges in their bodies.

Our pets can be great models for practicing line drawings. Because they move around so much, they force us to draw quickly and freely and not to get too uptight about our finished products.

Just like apples, there are lots of circles and ovals in cats.

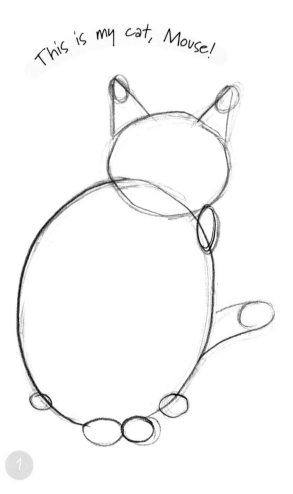

This is my cat, Mouse!

1

2

More Cats

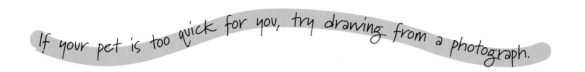

If your pet is too quick for you, try drawing from a photograph.

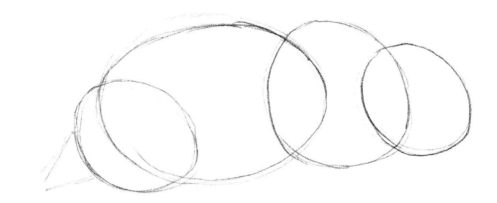

1

Meow!

For Dog Lovers

Practice drawing my dog. She may not look as curvy as a cat, but once you train your artist's eyes, you'll be able to spot bulges and curves in almost any animal.

After drawing this photograph, try drawing your own pet. Hamsters, rabbits, and even lizards and snakes make great models. If you don't have any pets, try drawing from pictures of animals in magazines, or try sketching squirrels and birds in your backyard or at the park.

Next, you'll learn how to add cool shadows and highlights...

Chapter Three

Light and Shadow

If it weren't for light, we wouldn't see anything at all. If it weren't for shadows, things would always look flat or two-dimensional. To make our drawings look as realistic as possible (or three-dimensional), we need to recognize that an object's shadows really define the shape of that object.

Artists translate shadow into *values*—different tones ranging from the blackest black to the whitest white, along with all the shades of gray in between. These simple tones add life to your drawings.

Can you find the shadows in this photograph?

Try drawing this mug with its shadows.

Value Scales

The bars below (called *value scales*) show many of the different ways you can represent shadow with your pencil. The first block in each value scale is white. The last block is the darkest value. After the first block, each tone is a little darker than the one before it.

Smooth Shading: Try to keep your pencil marks blended together.

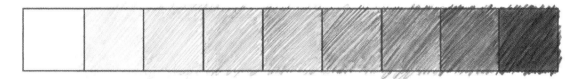

Hatching: Make a series of parallel lines. To make your hatched shadows darker, press down on your pencil harder, and draw the lines closer together.

Cross-hatching: Make a series of crisscrossed lines.

Stippling: Make a series of dots. Your dotted shadow will look darker if you press down harder on your pencil and place the dots closer together.

Scribbling: I'm sure you know how to scribble.

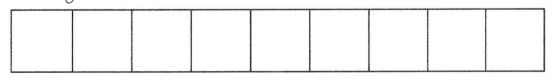

Trace this blank value scale in your sketchbook a bunch of times, and practice each of these shading techniques. Try to keep your changes in value steady.

Finding and Drawing Shadows

Go into a dim room with two pencils and your drawing paper. Turn on a table lamp. This lamp should be the only strong light source in the room. If there's a lot of light coming through the windows, close the blinds. With your nondrawing hand (I'm going to call this hand your modeling hand), hold a pencil by the eraser and place the tip on the paper. Look at the shadow cast on the paper where the light falls over the pencil. Notice the angle of the shadow. How many different values can you see?

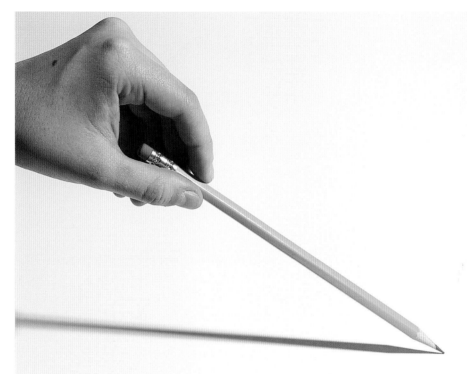

1 Draw the pencil you're holding in your modeling hand. Finding the simple shapes within the pencil should be a breeze for you by now.

2 Look at the long part of the pencil. What values do you see? Notice how the surface closest to the light source is lighter and how the surface farthest away from it is darker. Draw these values, and add shading to the cone-shaped pencil tip. Sketch in the basic shape of the cast shadow.

3 Observe the shape and value of the cast shadow. Is it similar in shape to the pencil or is it more stretched out? Is it long and skinny or shorter and fatter than the pencil? Notice how it's darkest where it's closest to the tip and how the outside edges of the shadow are lighter and fuzzier than the inside.

Turn on the overhead light and try this again.

How are the shadows different with more than one light source?

Shadows on Spheres

Find a ball or other spherical object and go back to your dim room with the table lamp. Place the ball on the table and adjust your light source so it's shining down on the ball at an angle.

Take a minute to observe the shape of the shadow. Where are the darkest areas on the ball? Where are the lightest areas? Where are the middle gray tones?

Now try drawing it.

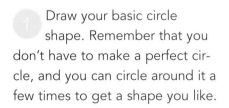

1 Draw your basic circle shape. Remember that you don't have to make a perfect circle, and you can circle around it a few times to get a shape you like.

2 Find the dark shadow areas on the ball first. Sketch in the dark and dark-medium values a shade or two lighter at first. You can always go darker later.

3 Now find the medium-dark tones.

4 Find the medium-light tones. Make sure you keep the highlighted (lightest) areas white.

Use the value scales you drew from page 35 to keep your changes in value steady.

5 Finally, emphasize the darkest darks and cast the shadow. Notice that the cast shadow is darkest where it's closest to the ball. You may want to use the corner of your eraser to lift off any graphite that got on the highlight.

See how I scribbled the background?

Multiple Light Sources

Now that you've gotten some practice drawing something with one light source, try this: set an empty toilet paper tube in the lighting situation you set up on page 36, and turn on the overhead light. Now that you have more than one light source, your light and shadows are going to look very different.

Hey, why are you drawing a toilet paper tube? First of all, there is a simple beauty to the shape. When you see the world with your artist's eyes, you'll find elegance and grace in the most common objects. Second, tubes are an incredibly useful building block in drawing. They will help you later when you draw trees and people.

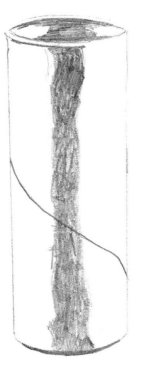 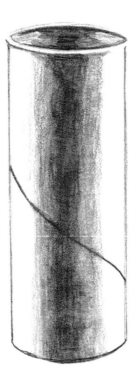 

1. Draw the tube. Find the darkest darks on the tube. Because this tube is lit from both sides, the darkest darks are in the center.

2. Next, find and draw the medium-light tones.

3. Draw the medium-dark tones.

Now draw the tube from lots of different angles.

4 Finally, cast your shadows. The light source to the left of my tube is stronger than the one on the right. That's why the shadow cast to the right of the tube is darker and more prominent than the one on the left.

The background can be a very important part of a drawing. In this drawing, the tube is resting on a white surface against a gray wall. The medium gray of the background helps define the shape of the tube; it provides contrast to the very light sides of the tube.

Now practice drawing a full roll of toilet paper.

Unroll some of the paper and draw the delicate folds. I love exploring the gentle folds and curves of the paper cascading from the roll. And this kind of observation is an incredible skill builder. It's great practice for a future challenge: drawing the fabric that you see in clothing.

Add Shading to Your Line Drawings

In Chapter 1 you drew several line drawings. Over the next few pages, you'll get to revisit those drawings so you can add some light and shadow to them.

After the sun has gone down, find a dimly lit room where you can draw comfortably while looking at the door you first drew on page 26. Turn on the light in the room behind the door. Open the door a foot or so. Spend some time observing the effects of the light on the door and the light and shadows cast on the floor of the room you're in. You may need to use a reading lamp so you can see your drawing better, but you don't want to turn on the overhead light. This will spoil the effect. The main light source should be coming from just behind the slightly opened the door.

1   Using simple straight lines, rectangles, and triangles, find the basic shape of your door as you did in chapter 2. Now, squint to see where the darkest shadows are in your composition. In my room, the darkest darks fell just outside the door frame.

2   Next, squint to see the medium-dark values on the wall and door frame. I used the cross-hatching shading technique from page 35.

3 Now, squint and take a long look at the range of values on the door itself. In this drawing, the door is almost like its very own value scale. The hinged edge is pretty dark, and the door gets lighter toward the edge as it gets closer to the light source. Sketch in the medium-light values on the inside of the door frame.

4 Sketch the angles of light and shadow cast through the door onto the floor.

5 Squint to see the different values of cast light and shadow. Are your shadows all one tone? Are there a variety of values? Draw them.

I used cross-hatching to add value to the wall!

Revisit Your Apple

Set an apple on the table in front of you and draw it using the technique you learned on page 27. Now, identify the direction of your main light source. In my drawing, the light source is coming from the upper right corner. Squint to see the patches of dark value. Sketch in the dark and medium-dark tones.

Now, sketch in the medium and medium light-tones. Notice how the values get lighter on the areas of the apple that are closer to the light source. Make sure to leave blank white areas where the highlights are.

Next, darken your dark tones and sharpen the detail. Did you add shading to the stem? Does the stem cast a shadow on the skin of the apple? Finally, add the shadow cast on the table. Notice how the shadow is darker in the center and lighter around the edges.

light source

I bet your apple looks yummier now!

Add Shading to Mouse the Cat

Remember my cat, Mouse, from page 28? Not only are we adding shading to make Mouse seem more three-dimensional, but we're paying attention to the kind of shading we're using in order to add texture. I used hatch marks that "grow" from her skin in the same direction that her hair does. Look at the shadows on her front legs and under her chin, for example. Also, I translated her orange and black markings into gray tones from the value scale (see page 35). With these values, I also hatched in the direction of hair growth to make her look soft and furry.

You can use shading to represent color and texture!

Drawing on Colored Paper

Up until now, you've been using a pencil to draw the darkest darks, the medium tones, and the light grays. You've left the paper blank to represent the lightest parts of the drawing.

Now try working on middle-tone drawing paper like I did with this pear. A middle-tone paper can be any color. (When you squint, it should be somewhere in the middle range of your value scale.) Instead of drawing the middle grays with a pencil, let the paper represent those values. In this drawing, I used a brown pastel to draw the shadows and a white pastel to draw the highlights (the brightest parts).

Use textured paper to pick up the pastel markings better.

Begin by lightly sketching the basic shapes within the pear. Next, add the skin. Find the darkest shadows on the pear. Don't make them too dark at first. (It's always easier to make things darker later than it is to lighten them up.)

Add the medium-dark shadows. Remember to leave blank areas for the medium tones.

Next, add highlights with the white pastel. Cast the shadow. Draw a line behind the fruit to suggest the edge of a table. Use shading in the background to emphasize the highlights on the pear. Do you see how I drew darker values on the light side of the pear? This punches up the highlights, giving the pear a more dramatic sense of volume. It also helps balance the light and dark areas of the drawing.

From Tubes to Trees

Remember the toilet paper tube you drew on pages 40 and 41? Here's where they really start to come in handy. When you're drawing the trunk and branches of a tree, it helps to see them as a series of interconnected tube shapes. Tree limbs bend and twist and branch off in different directions. Studying trees closely and piecing them together as tubes can help you draw their forms.

Then, as you add the connective "skin" over these tubes, you can focus on texture and shading. Does the tree have smooth bark? Is the bark divided into lots of blocky shapes or into long, narrow ridges? Does the tree have knots and bumps on its surface? When you add shadows, think back to the toilet paper roll: identify your light source and then cast your shadows.

Trees come in a variety of basic shapes. Some are cone shaped, others look like columns, and others look like big fluffy balls on a stick. Some are so irregular it would be impossible to reduce them to a simple geometric shape. Spend some time looking at trees and drawing their basic shapes.

When drawing a tree's leaves, it's important to use marks that express the kind of texture you want to capture. If you're drawing a pine tree, for exam-ple, you'll probably want to use small straight marks to show the pointy texture of the pine needles. For a big, fluffy maple tree, your marks may look more like squiggles. Pay close attention to value; squint to simplify the tree's leaves into blocks of value. Notice how some of the "clumps" of leaves are darker in value—perhaps they're closer to the trunk of the tree and farther away from the sun—and other clumps of leaves are lighter in value.

Chapter Four

Proportion and Scale

Proportion and scale are words we use to talk about relative size—the relationships between the sizes of different things. We say things are "out of proportion" when the size relationships in a drawing don't match the objects they're meant to represent.

Take a look at this photograph of a *still life*. (Still lifes are little scenes usually made up of common objects you find around the house.) Now, look at the two drawings I did of the still life. One is in proportion and the other isn't.

It's important to be able to get proportions right *if you want to*. Lots of artists choose to draw things out of proportion on purpose. Playing with proportions can be a fun way to achieve different effects.

There are zillions of size relationships like this everywhere you look. For example, in this still life, the vase is about two flowers tall. How many wheels wide is the skateboard? How many flowers long is the skateboard? You can also use your finger to measure if you want.

Notice how the size relationships between the photograph and this drawing are the same. For example, the height of the vase and flower is just about the same as the length of the skateboard. Also, the flower in the photo is just a little bit wider than the mouth of the vase.

This drawing is in proportion.

This drawing is out of proportion.

In this drawing, lots of things are out of proportion. See how the height of the vase and flower isn't nearly as long as the skateboard? And how the width of the flower isn't as wide as the mouth of the vase? Do you see other things in the drawing that are out of proportion?

The rest of this chapter shows you tricks to help you draw in proportion.

The Famous Pencil Trick

This is a great trick to help get proportions right. If you're drawing a friend playing guitar, you can't really measure everything with a ruler. The pencil trick lets you stay seated while checking the proportions in your drawing. In this example, I measured the width of the body of the guitar (the black and white part) and used that measurement to find the height of the girl.

Close one eye. It's important to look with only one eye; this makes your subject appear flatter, (more like a drawing itself) and makes it easier to measure. Identify an area of your subject that would make a good measurement. Choose something small or with clear edges. For this drawing, the body of the guitar is a good choice.

One unit!

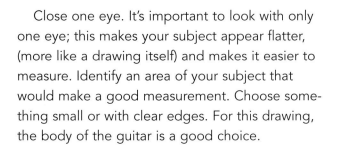

1. Extend your arm straight out toward your subject. Hold the pencil so the eraser is even with one edge of your subject. Here, it's even with the left edge of the guitar. Place your thumb on the pencil to mark the other edge of what you're measuring. Keep your thumb on this spot or make a pen mark. Here, I measured the body of the guitar, from the left edge to where it meets the neck. This measurement is one unit. Use this unit to measure other parts of your subject.

2. Extend your arm again; line the eraser up with a different edge of your subject. Here, it's even with the top of the girl's head. Notice where your thumb-held mark hits the subject. Here, it's even with the girl's armpit. Make a mental note of this spot.

Proportion and

③ Move the eraser down to meet the next spot. Again, note where the mark hits the subject. Here, it falls at her fingertips.

④ Move your pencil down again, lining the eraser up to this next spot. The mark hits the subject at the bottom of her straight knee.

⑤ Continue this process until you've reached another edge. Keep track of how many units you've counted. Here, the girl is four units tall, from the top of her head to the bottom of her shoe. Sometimes measurements won't work out perfectly and you can guesstimate. In this picture, for example, the whole guitar is a little less than two-and-a-half units long.

You'll learn to draw people in Chapters 6 and 7.

Dollhouse or Real House?

If the house in this drawing is supposed to be the girl's home, we would say that it's out of proportion. It would be way too small for her to fit her backpack in, let alone a bedroom, kitchen ... But as a dollhouse it's just fine—it's in proportion.

Chapter 5 will show you how to draw the path.

What about this drawing? If the girl took a walk down that path toward the house, she would be able to open up the door and walk right in.

If you measure with your pencil, you'll see that the house and the girl in both of the drawings are exactly the same size. How can this be? When we look into the distance, things farther away appear smaller than they actually are. The second drawing is composed in such a way that the house appears to be far away, or in the background, and the girl appears to be close up, or in the foreground.

Using Grids to Draw in Proportion

For hundreds of years artists have used grids as a drawing tool to help keep things in proportion. The idea is simple: by viewing your subject through a grid, you reduce it into smaller, more manageable segments. You transfer the information you see in each of these squares into a corresponding square on your paper. The grid on your paper may be the exact same size as the one on the photograph. It can also be larger or smaller. As long as the grid on your paper is composed of the same number of squares (not rectangles!) as the one on your photo, you'll be able to keep the composition in proportion as you reduce or enlarge it.

Find a photograph that's okay to draw on. You can also use a photocopy or printed scan of the photograph or a picture from a magazine. Use a ruler and a ballpoint pen to draw a grid of squares over your photo.

Now, using a pencil and a ruler, draw a grid of squares on your paper. Remember, the squares you draw on your paper can be smaller than, the same size as, or larger than the ones you drew on your photo. Moving square by square, begin transferring the information from your photo onto your paper. Check the placement of your lines by noticing where they fall in relation to the sides of the square.

Out-of-Proportion Gridding

Sometimes you may not want your drawing to reflect the exact proportions of the subject. You can use the grid technique to distort your drawing.

Draw a grid of squares over your photograph. But this time, instead of drawing squares on your paper, draw rectangles. If you want to have a short, squatty drawing of your original subject, draw horizontal rectangles. If you want to have a tall, skinny drawing of your subject, draw vertical rectangles.

Transfer the information from each of the squares on your photo into the corresponding rectangle on your paper. If a line in the original falls a little less than halfway across a side of a square, then it will fall a little less than halfway across the side of the corresponding rectangle. The rectangles act as a guide to help you stretch the proportions of your drawing.

Use distorted grids to make funny faces!

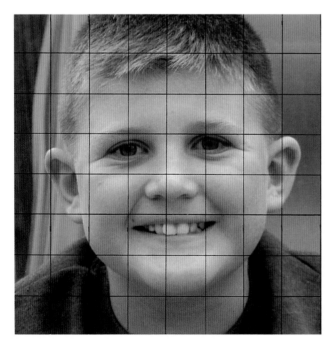

Foreshortening

When an object is pointing toward the viewer, it appears to be much shorter than it actually is. We say that it's *foreshortened*. Also, the part of the object closest to the viewer appears much larger than it really is.

Take a look at the girl below. Look how her arm appears shorter as she moves it toward you. In which photo does her hand look the largest?

You can use the pencil trick on page 52 or a grid (see page 55) to check the length of something that's foreshortened.

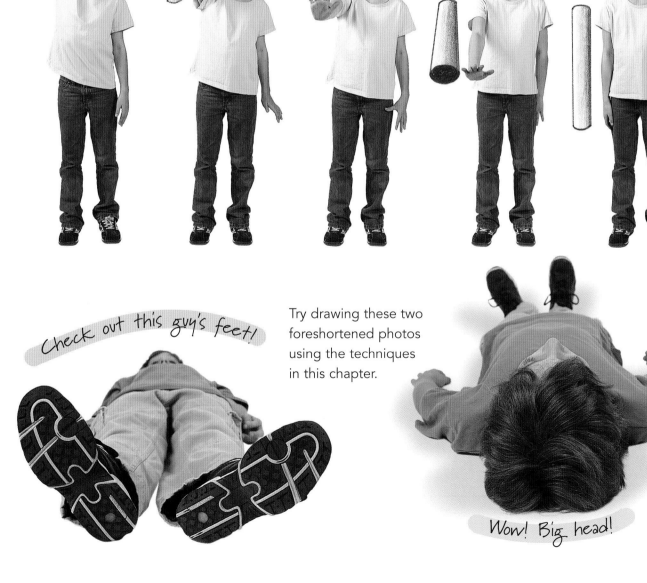

Practice drawing foreshorted tubes.

Check out this guy's feet!

Try drawing these two foreshortened photos using the techniques in this chapter.

Wow! Big head!

Perspective

Have you ever stared at a long, flat highway? Did you notice how the edges of the road and the lines painted on the road look like they all meet at a dot in the distance? This illusion is part of what's called *linear perspective*. You can re-create this illusion on paper when you draw a long road, shooting stars heading right for you, a hallway, rows of corn in a cornfield, a tree, a table—pretty much anything with right angles that moves back into space.

The tricks of linear perspective are based on a couple of visual illusions. The first is that things appear smaller as they move farther away from you. The second is that parallel lines appear to get closer together as they get farther away from you. For example, look at the school hallway on the right. If you use a ruler to extend all the lines that are moving back into space, you'll find that they all meet up at one point. This point is called the *vanishing point*. The lines that extend back into space are called *perspective lines*. The vanishing point rests on a line that moves straight across the page. This is called the *horizon line*.

See how the lines get closer together as they move farther away.

Perspective lines

Horizon line

Vanishing point

There are visible and invisible lines pointing toward vanishing points everywhere you look.

The Rules of One-Point Perspective

I used the rules of one-point perspective to draw these shelves and books. Two of the shelves are above the horizon line, one is at the horizon line, and the other two are below the horizon line.

Because the edges of the books are parallel with the sides of the shelves, they all move back toward the same vanishing point. Even the edges of the individual pages and the middle line of the book refer to the same vanishing point.

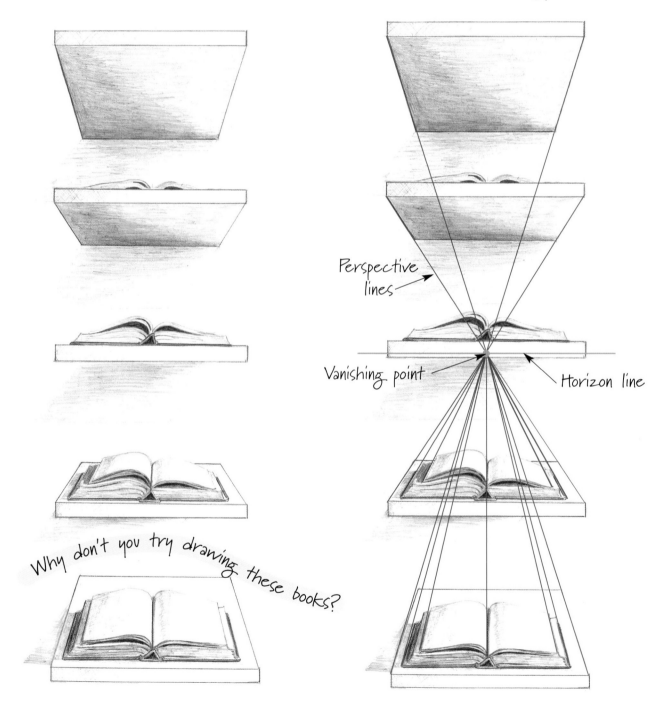

Perspective lines

Vanishing point

Horizon line

Why don't you try drawing these books?

Find the Vanishing Point

This drawing also follows the rules of one-point perspective. Can you find the vanishing point? Do you see how the sides of the drawers, the edges of the room, and all the boards in the floor point back toward the vanishing point?

Look around your own room and find a one-point perspective scene to draw. Remember, you need to be square to your subject. If you're drawing your dresser, for example, you'll want to face it straight on, not from one of its corners.

Turn to page 111 if you're having trouble finding the vanishing point.

61

Drawing with One-Point Perspective

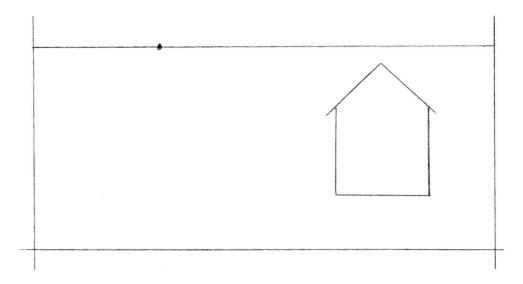

1 Draw a horizon line. You can place it high up on the paper, near the middle, or down low. Draw the vanishing point on the horizon line. Next, draw a box for the house. Don't forget the roof.

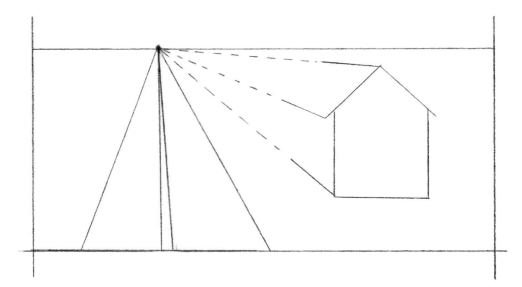

2 Use the ruler to draw a road extending from the vanishing point up into the foreground of the drawing. Now, draw lines connecting the edges of the house to the vanishing point. Make sure you connect the bottom edge of the square closest to the vanishing point, and the bottom and top edges of the roof.

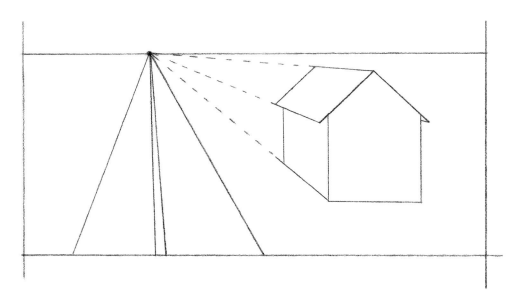

3 Draw the back edges of the house. These lines are parallel to other corresponding lines in the drawing—so the back edge of the house will be parallel to the front edge of the house and the back edge of the roof will be parallel to the front edge of the roof.

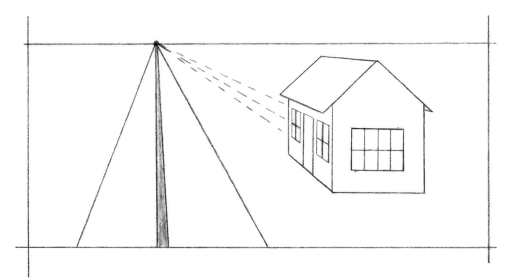

4 Draw lines to the vanishing point that will mark the top of the door and the tops and bottoms of the windows. The sides of the windows and doors will be parallel to the sides of the house.

Flying at Ya!

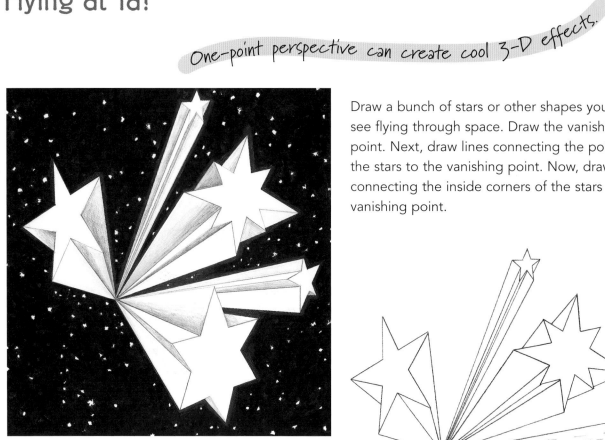

Draw a bunch of stars or other shapes you'd like to see flying through space. Draw the vanishing point. Next, draw lines connecting the points of the stars to the vanishing point. Now, draw lines connecting the inside corners of the stars to the vanishing point.

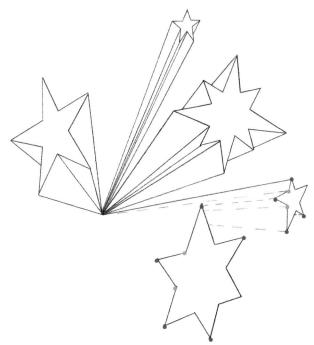

Imagine your name in lights!

An Ant's Eye-View

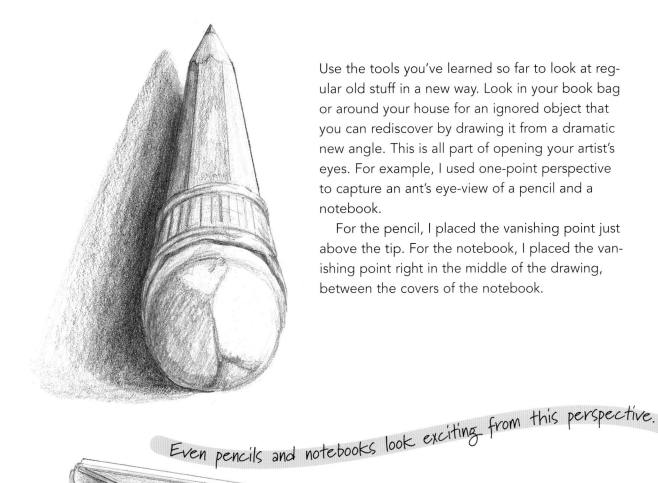

Use the tools you've learned so far to look at regular old stuff in a new way. Look in your book bag or around your house for an ignored object that you can rediscover by drawing it from a dramatic new angle. This is all part of opening your artist's eyes. For example, I used one-point perspective to capture an ant's eye-view of a pencil and a notebook.

For the pencil, I placed the vanishing point just above the tip. For the notebook, I placed the vanishing point right in the middle of the drawing, between the covers of the notebook.

Even pencils and notebooks look exciting from this perspective.

Two-Point Perspective

Two-point perspective is just what it sounds like: instead of using one vanishing point, you're using two. With one-point perspective, you were drawing things with pretty simple angles. Your subject was square with the viewer and with the edges of the page. Now, with two-point perspective, you can draw things at much more complicated angles.

Take a look at this city building. Use a ruler to mark how the edges of the building extend back into space. The places where these lines intersect are the vanishing points.

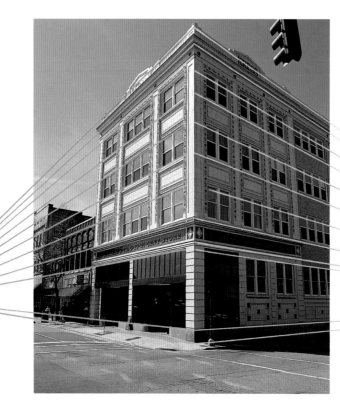

Getting Started with Two-Point Perspective

1. Begin by drawing your horizon line. Now, instead of one vanishing point, draw two. Next, draw a vertical line that crosses the horizon line somewhere between these two points.

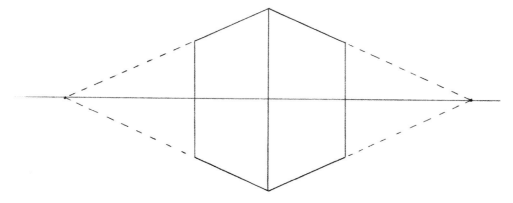

2. With a ruler, connect the top and bottom of the vertical line to the two vanishing points. Finally, draw the back edges of your box.

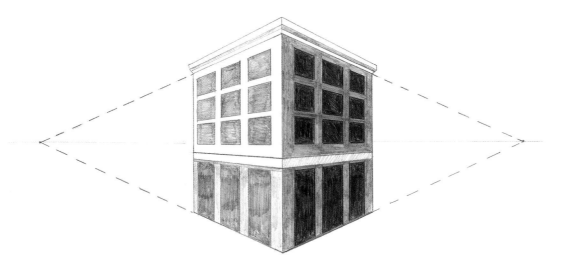

3. Transforming this box into a building is simply a matter of adding detail. Use the two vanishing points to add doors and windows.

More Fun with Two-Point Perspective

Keep practicing basic two-point perspective. What does it look like if you draw a box above, at, or beow the horizon line? How does it change things if you draw the box toward the right or left sides of the page?

If you can draw a box in perspective, then you can draw all sorts of things such as rooms, beds, computers, and more.

It's simple to transform a box into a chair.

Now take it a step further: use two-point perspective to add thickness and detail to your chair. Then erase your perspective lines.

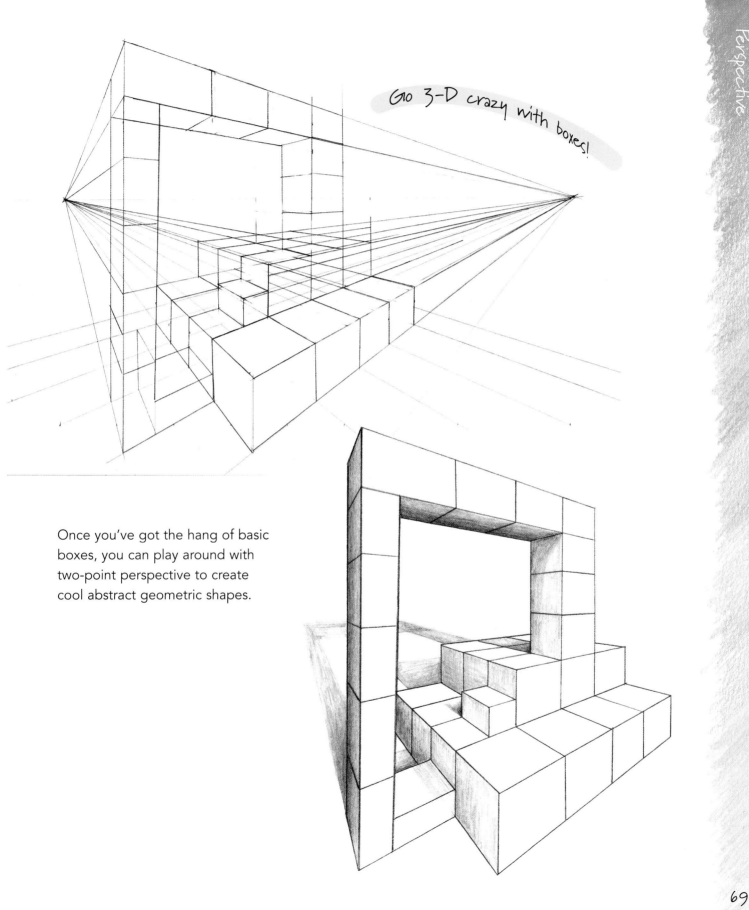

Go 3-D crazy with boxes!

Once you've got the hang of basic boxes, you can play around with two-point perspective to create cool abstract geometric shapes.

69

Draw a Basketball Court

The cool thing about drawing a gym is that there are many parallel lines and right angles, so lots of lines in the picture refer to one of the vanishing points.

1 Draw a horizon line and two vanishing points. It helps to imagine that the horizon line is actually outside the building. Next draw the vertical line that marks the corner of the gymnasium and the two lines that mark where each of the two walls meets the floor.

horizon line

2 Draw the outline of the basketball court.

3 Draw the markings on the court. If you have trouble drawing the circles, remember this: circles fit inside squares. Use your vanishing points to draw a square on the floor and then draw the circle to fit inside it. Then draw the hoops.

4　For the bleachers, use the right vanishing point to get the angles right for the tops of the steps. Use the left vanishing point for the long front edges of the bleachers as well as the top and bottom edges of the windows.

Three-Point Perspective

To draw something in three-point perspective, start off just like you did for two-point perspective. The difference is that all of the lines that were parallel to the sides of the page in two-point perspective will now refer to the third vanishing point.

If you want the effect to be that you're looking up at your subject, place the third vanishing point above the horizon line.

Three-point perspective is just what it sounds like.

See how this drawing makes you feel small?

Look what happens when you place the third vanishing-point below the horizon line.

Draw a Landscape

Landscape drawing can be fun and challenging because you might be fitting miles of space onto a piece of paper. In the landscape below, I used these tricks of what's called *atmospheric perspective* to create the illusion of open space:

- Things get fuzzier the farther away they are.
- Things tend to appear lighter in value the farther away they are.
- Things appear to get smaller the farther away they are.
- Things appear closer together the farther away they are.

Notice how I used darker lines and added more detail for the grass in the foreground. The grass gets lighter and less detailed the farther away it is.

For the foreground, use a sharp pencil. Make crisp lines and add lots of detail. For the background, use a dull pencil to make soft marks. You can use your finger to smudge the edges to make things look soft and smoky. For objects in the middle (the middle ground), use a pencil that's slightly dull. If your pencil's too sharp, scribble back and forth on scrap paper until the tip is rounded.

The lines in nature aren't hard and crisp the way they are in buildings and boxes, but you can still use linear perspective to help you when drawing a landscape.

For each section of the waterway, I connected the edges to a point on the horizon. For each turn, I chose a different point on the horizon than the one before. This is the same technique I used to draw the zigzagged pathway on page 54. I rounded out the curves to make it look more natural.

I've exaggerated the effect here to show you how even fluffy, unpredictable clouds loosely follow the rules of perspective; they get smaller and closer together as they move toward the horizon into the distance.

Chapter Six

Drawing Faces

People often say that faces are about the hardest things to draw. As with snowflakes, no two faces are exactly alike. If you look closely you'll notice that even the faces of identical twins have differences. The endless variety of the human face makes it even more amazing that most faces follow some basic rules of proportion and shape. Once you learn these basic rules, drawing faces isn't really any harder than drawing the objects in the last four chapters. The idea is the same: you identify the simple shapes and lines in the face and put them together.

Faces are chock-full of circles, ovals, and simple curves.

The Face Map

First, the basic shape of the human head is eggish. Look in a mirror and use the pencil-measuring trick on page 52 to measure the length and width of your face. You'll find that your face is longer than it is wide.

Sure there are variations—some people have round cheeks, some have square jaws—but for now we'll start with the basic egg shape.

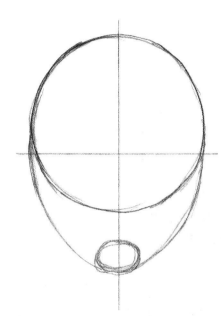

1 Draw a circle—this is the brain circle. It marks the shape of the top part of the head—the part of the skull that holds the brain.

Now draw a small circle centered and a little below the first one. This is the chin circle.

2 Now use two curved lines to connect the circles into an egg shape.

3 Next, draw a vertical line straight down the middle of the face. This line will help you keep your nose and mouth centered and the right and left sides of your face symmetrical.

Now draw another line that divides the face into upper and lower halves. This is the eye line, and it will help you draw the eyes in the right place.

The eyes are actually located in the middle of the face!

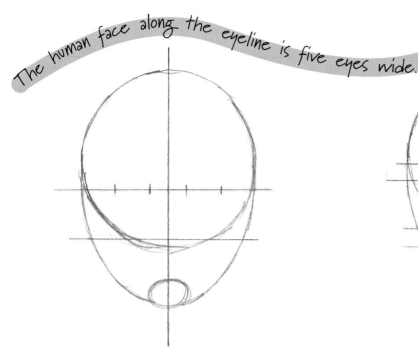

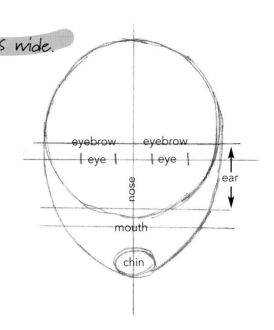

The human face along the eyeline is five eyes wide.

eyebrow   eyebrow
| eye | | eye |
nose
ear
mouth
chin

4 Divide the eye line into five equal sections. If you look in the mirror, you can see that the space between your eyes—not just the bridge of your nose, but the space from tear duct to tear duct—is about the same width as one of your eyes. You can also see that the space from the outside edge of your eye to the side of your temple is also about one eye wide.

5 Draw a line about halfway between the eye line and the bottom of the chin. This will be the guideline for the nose. The nostrils will fall a little bit above this line. Draw a line a little bit below the nose line. This will be the guideline for the mouth. Finally, draw a line a little bit above the eye line. This line will show you where the eyebrows should go and where the top of the ears will be. This is your face map.

See how funny it looks when the eyes are drawn where the forehead should be? Look in the mirror and, using the pencil trick on page 52 or an actual ruler, measure the distance between your eyes and your chin and between your eyes and the very top of your head (not your hairline). Your eyes, like most everyone else's, are right in the middle of your face.

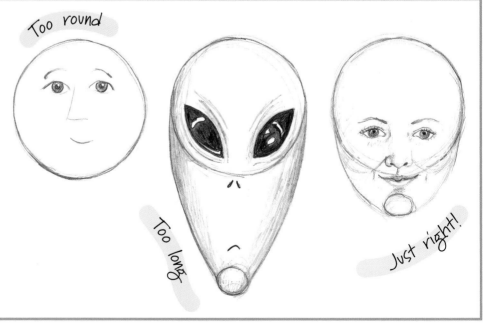

Too round

Too long

Just right!

How Faces Change

The face map varies according to the age of the subject. The eyes of a baby, for instance, are lower on the face. The tops of the eyes fall just below the eye line. A baby's nose is also shorter than an adult's. As the face grows older, the eyes move up on the face, moving closer to the eye line, and the nose gets longer.

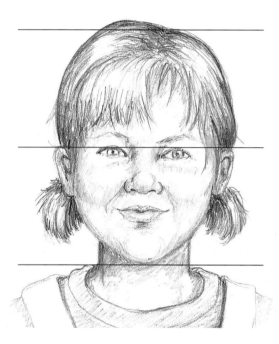

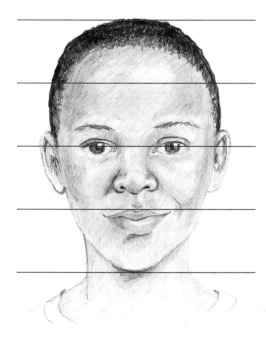

Eyes and Nose and Mouth and Ears

If you can draw the shapes in the colored boxes, you can draw a face!

Eyes

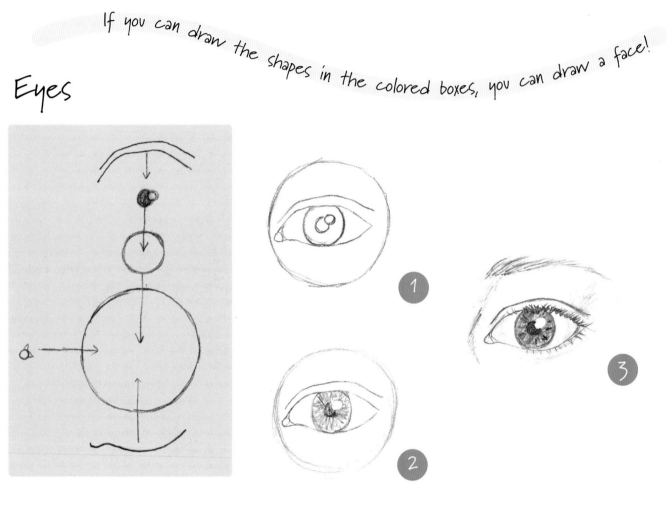

Nose

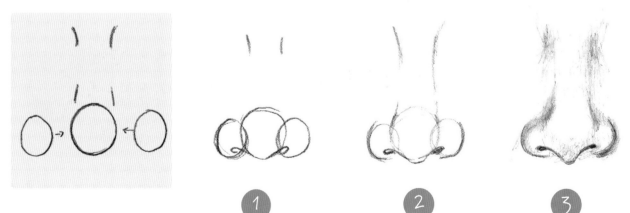

Mouth

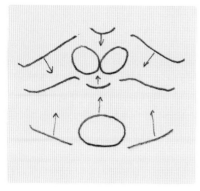

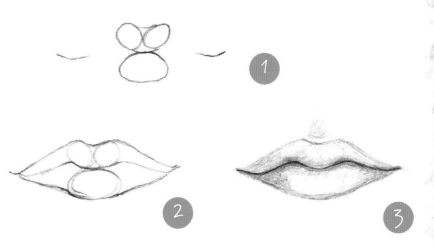

Ears

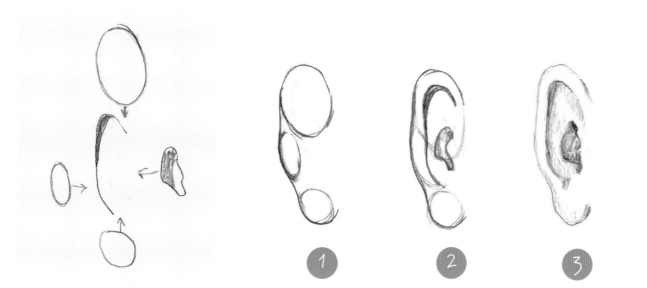

Draw a Face

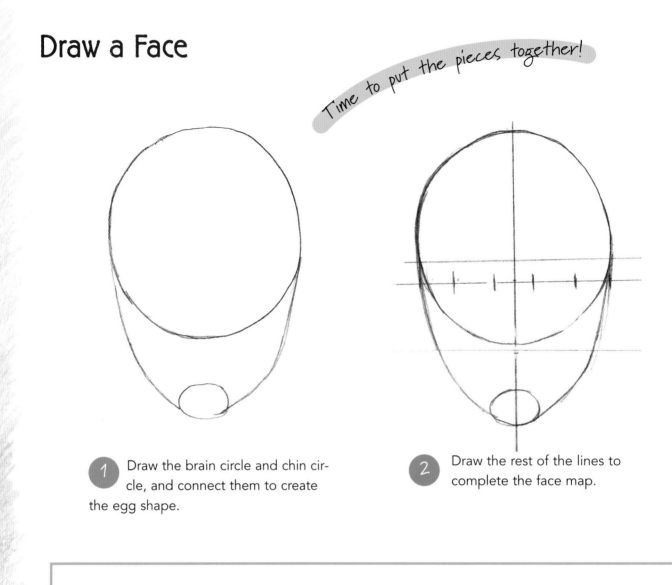

1 Draw the brain circle and chin circle, and connect them to create the egg shape.

2 Draw the rest of the lines to complete the face map.

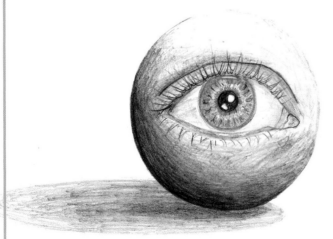

Even though we see only a small portion of the eyeball when we look at a person's face, it's important to remember that there is a perfectly round eyeball resting in the eye socket beneath layers of skin and muscle.

Remembering this helps us draw the fold of the eyelid so that it looks more realistic. It also helps us place the shadow beneath the eye.

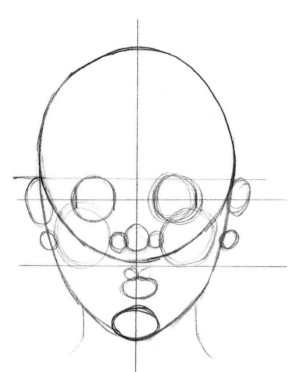

3 Draw two circles where the eyes will go. Draw the circular shapes that make up the nose, cheekbones, ears, lips, and chin.

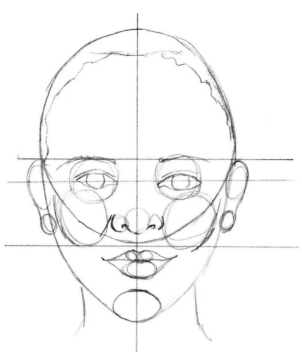

4 Sketch the hairline. Draw the shapes of the eyelids and eyebrows. Refine the shape of the nose.

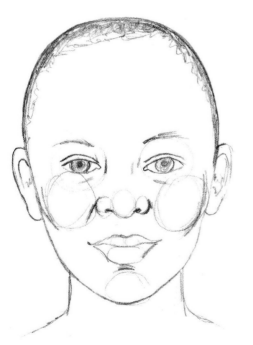

5 Use your eraser to soften some of your guidelines. Identify the direction of the light source.

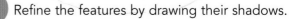

6 Refine the features by drawing their shadows.

Draw a Profile

In some ways profiles are easier to draw than frontal views of faces. With the previous drawing, you had to make sure the nose didn't look flat, so you created the illusion of depth with shadow. With a profile, all you have to do is draw the length of the nose. You don't have to worry so much about creating an illusion.

1 Draw the brain circle and the chin circle. Sketch in a curved jawline to connect them.

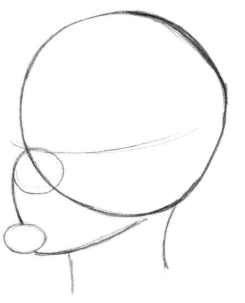

2 Identify the eye line. Sketch in the circle for the cheekbone and then draw the curved line that marks the front slope of the cheek.

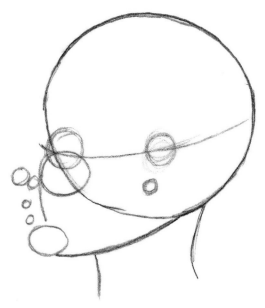

3 Draw the circles for the eye, nose, and lips. Draw the circles for the ear. (The ear is between the brow line and the bottom of the nose.)

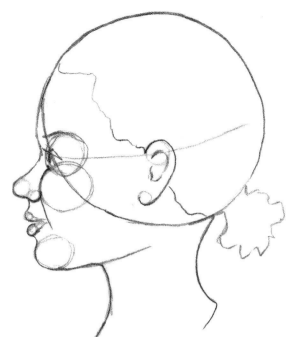

Turn to page 88 for more on drawing hair.

4 Use small curved lines to define the features. Pay attention to the eyelid, nostril, and lips. Draw the hairline.

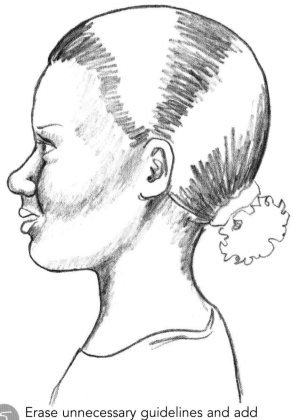

5 Erase unnecessary guidelines and add shading to the drawing.

6 Continue shading to create skin tones. Don't forget to create highlights as well.

The Three-Quarter View

This drawing shows a three-quarter view. When drawing a face from this angle, the chin circle will be off-center, the eye line will be curved to show the curve of the face, and the lines marking the placement of the nose and mouth will also be curved.

1 Begin the drawing in the same way—by identifying the brain circle and the chin circle.

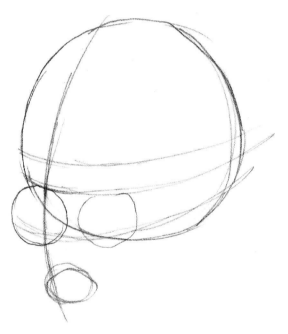

2 Draw the eye line and the nose line. Draw circles for the cheeks.

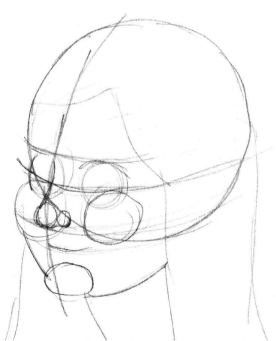

3 Draw the circles for the eyes, nose, and ear (unless the ear is hidden by hair as it is here). Draw the hairline.

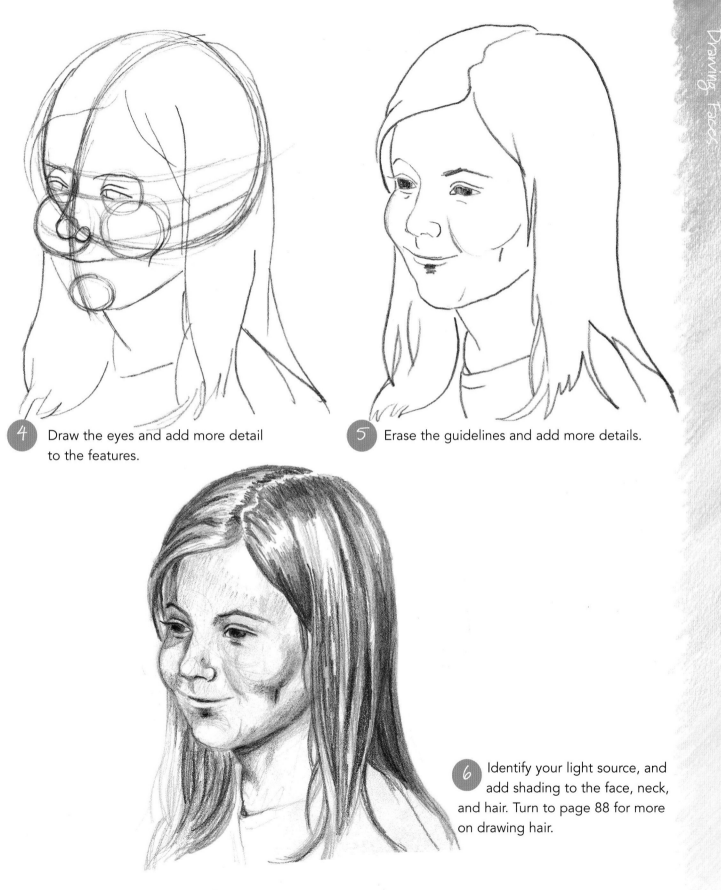

4 Draw the eyes and add more detail to the features.

5 Erase the guidelines and add more details.

6 Identify your light source, and add shading to the face, neck, and hair. Turn to page 88 for more on drawing hair.

Hair

One of the most important things to pay attention to when drawing hair is texture. Hair can be straight, wavy, curly, stringy, puffy, smooth, or frizzy, and the marks you make should reflect the texture you're trying to capture.

Draw lines in the same direction in which the hair grows. If you're drawing hair in a ponytail, your marks should follow the round shape of the skull.

When drawing hair in great detail, build up layers of line. In this example on the right, I started by defining the shape of the curl with a series of gray lines and then defined the shadows of the curl with darker lines.

Whether you're drawing blonde, brown, gray, red, black, or purple hair, you're going to use a range of values (see page 35). Even the blackest hair reflects light and will have lighter areas that make the hair look shiny and real.

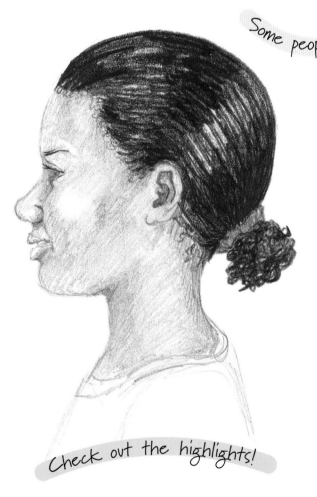

Some people have a whole value scale of tones in their hair.

Check out the highlights!

Expressions

Notice how different features move on the face to show emotions or personality traits.

Playful

Excited

Disappointed

Goofy

Chapter Seven

Drawing Bodies

Bodies, like faces, follow some basic guidelines of proportion. The body of a toddler, for example, is about four heads high. That is, if you stacked four of the toddler's heads on top of one another, they would be about as tall as the toddler. A preteen is about six heads high. An adult is seven or eight heads high, and a superhero (superheroes are so cool to draw!) is about nine heads high.

A person's shoulders are about one and a half heads wide.

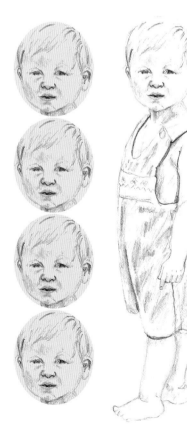

Body Building

Remember the toilet paper tubes and spheres you drew in Chapter 3? Those simple shapes will help you draw the human body.

Look at these figures. Their necks, arms, torsos, and legs are all a series of tubes. The hips, shoulders, and elbows—all of the joints—are made out of spheres. When you draw a torso, it helps to think of it as a slightly flattened toilet paper roll. If the figure's waist is smaller than the shoulders, you can think of the torso as a sort of flattened paper cup.

Study these figures and notice how the tubes and spheres fit together to make different gestures. All of your practice drawing foreshortened toilet paper rolls will pay off when you draw a figure with foreshortened limbs—such as the girl sitting down with her legs crossed.

Ta dah!

Drawing Bodies

Place tracing paper over these two photos and practice drawing spheres and tubes.

More Body Building

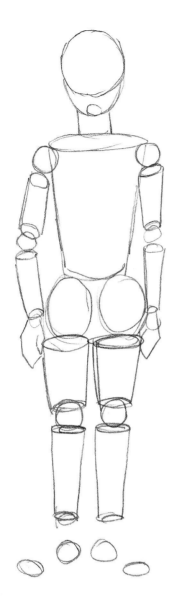

1 Time to build a body for yourself. Draw the head shape. Follow with a small tube for the neck and a large flattened tube (or paper cup) for the torso. Draw spheres and tubes for the rest of the body parts, including the feet.

2 Once you've drawn the basic shapes, soften the edges by drawing the "skin" over them.

If you can add shading to spheres and tubes, then this will be a cinch!

3 Dress your figure. Pay attention to the way the fabric falls over the body shapes. It's important to draw the basic shape of the body before dressing the figure. This way, you'll pay closer attention to proportion and make sure that the bulge of a knee through blue jeans or the bend of an elbow in a sweatshirt is in the right spot.

4 Once you've sketched the basic clothes and features of your figure, identify the light source and shade the drawing. Keep thinking about the figure in terms of spheres and tubes. You've already learned how to add shading to these simple shapes, and you can apply the same techniques when you shade the figure.

Draw Your Arm

Now you're ready to start adding more shape and definition to your figure. You do this by identifying the oval shapes in the arms and legs that represent muscles.

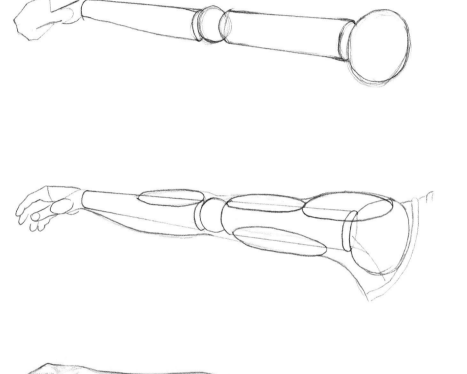

1 Look in a mirror and hold your arm out to the side. Notice where your upper arm bulges, the shape of your shoulder, and the curves of your forearm. Draw what you see with tubes and spheres.

2 Next, add long ovals to mark the bulges and curves of the flesh and muscles.

3 Finish up by softening the edges between these shapes and add "skin" to the arm. Erase any extra marks.

See page 98 for tips on drawing hands.

Pump It Up

1 Now, look in the mirror at your arm while it's flexed. Squeeze your muscles as hard as you can and notice how different they look. Draw the spheres and tubes of the shoulder and arm.

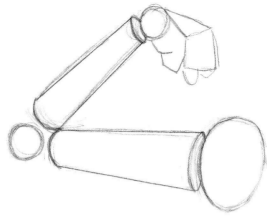

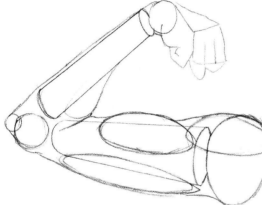

2 You may find that the long, skinny ovals and subtle curves you used the first time are replaced by rounder ovals and more dramatic curves.

3 Finish up by softening the edges between these shapes, and add "skin" to the arm. Don't forget to find your light source and add shading.

Think about the ways muscles move over the skeleton when you draw bodies in different positions. If you're drawing a baseball player throwing a ball, her arm muscles will look very different than they would if you were drawing the same person reading in a chair.

Hands Made Easy

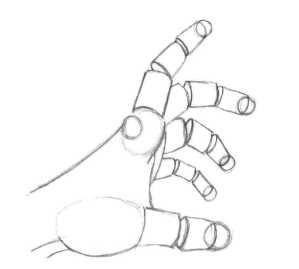

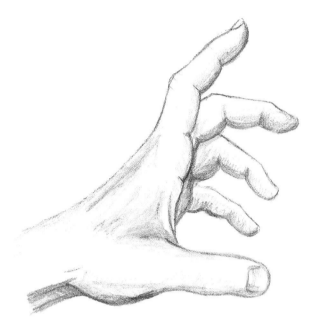

Hands can also be understood as a collection of simpler shapes. Each finger has three segments that are essentially tubes. The knuckles and fingertips can be simplified into sphere shapes.

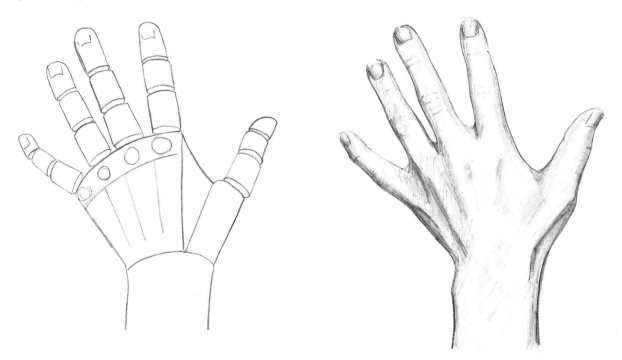

The back of the hand has tendons that stretch from each knuckle toward the wrist.

Hands can be as expressive as faces.

The great thing about drawing hands is that you don't have to ask someone to model for you. All you have to do is pose your nondrawing hand however you like it and draw.

The palm of the hand is fleshier and has more muscle than the top of the hand.

Legs

For more practice drawing the shape of flesh and muscle on the body, try looking at your legs in the mirror. Draw what they look like with the muscles relaxed. Try it again with your leg muscles flexed.

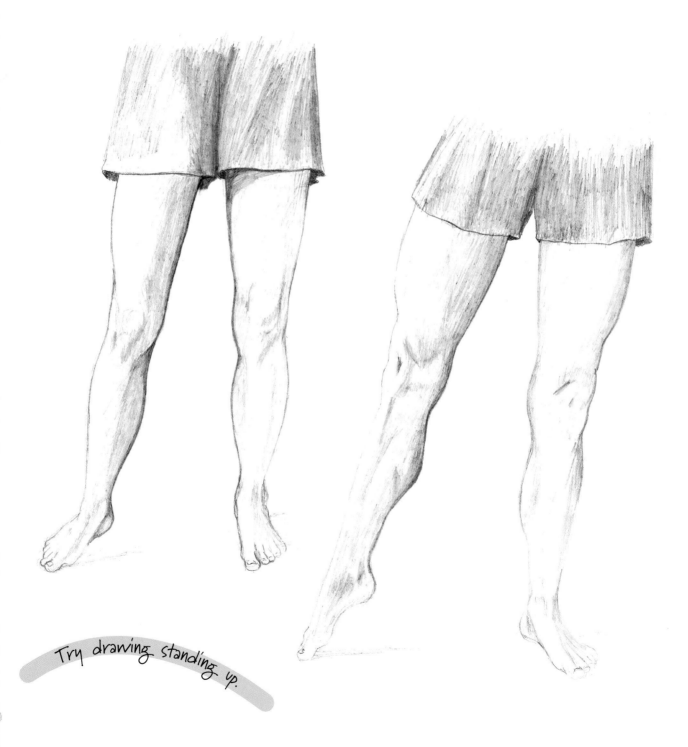

Try drawing standing up.

Gesture Drawing

Once you feel comfortable drawing the human form, you'll really enjoy *gesture drawing*. In gesture drawing, the artist uses quick and fluid movements to create the drawing. The end result is something lively and spontaneous—a drawing that may, even if it's not "accurate," represent the feeling of the moment much better than a carefully studied drawing that would take hours to do. Gesture drawings are especially beautiful when capturing a subject that's in motion. Don't worry about things being just right; the feeling of the drawing is the most important part. Also don't feel like you need to erase mistakes. Those stray marks and sketched shapes are like a map of your drawing journey.

Give gesture drawing a whirl!

Chapter Eight

Anything Can Happen

The imagination is like soil—it's mysterious and fertile and the source of all kinds of life. Everything that's alive has the dirt to thank. Without it there would be no trees (no air) and no fruit and vegetables (no food). And without the imagination there would be no art. Anybody who has ever made mudpies or planted a flower knows that the soil can be fun, messy, wormy, slimy, and sometimes even a little bit creepy. Like our imaginations and our dreams, soil is dark and mysterious, and we don't always know what's down there.

Part of the beauty of drawing a picture, as opposed to taking a photograph, is that anything can happen. If you want to draw a miniature staircase that leads right down into the earth, into the fertile soil of your imagination, no problem.

This final chapter is about creating drawings using your imagination and dreams as inspiration. Simply use the tools, tricks, and techniques you've learned in this book, add a little sprinkle or two of daydreaming, and see what happens.

Draw Your Imagination

Draw an imaginative self-portrait.

Create a life form.

Draw a feeling.

Draw an Imaginary Portrait Of Your Best Friend

Is your best friend funny and clever? Is he so great he seems to have magical powers? Like he could almost fly to the top of a telephone wire by the power of his wit and imagination?

Maybe he should have faerie wings.

Tips for Drawing Clouds

On a sunny day, spend some time lying in the grass looking up at the clouds. Notice all the different shapes they make. Sometimes they're big fluffy masses all lumped together; sometimes they're tiny puffs dotted across the sky. Squint your eyes to see the different values. Usually, the blue sky is a darker value than most of the clouds.

At first glance, the clouds may all seem to be the whitest white, but if you look more carefully, you'll probably find that there are lots of value variations.

To make the clouds fluffy and soft looking, use the side of your pencil rather than the hard tip. This way you can make soft patches of value, rather than sharp lines, to mark the edges of the cloud.

Water Reflections

I drew this picture after parts of my hometown were flooded by hurricane rains. Although it was sad to see so many buildings flooded, the scene itself was rather beautiful. The road completely disappeared under all the water, and everything—the buildings, the telephone poles, the clouds—was reflected in it. I drew the scene as I remembered it and added elements from my imagination.

It may seem difficult to draw a waterscape. It's hard just to describe the color of water. I mean, it's clear, right? But, the next time you're at a pond or a lake, spend some time looking at the landscape. If you live in a city and rarely see a large body of water, try this with a big puddle. Really.

Squint your eyes and look at the water's surface. Note all the colors you see. On a bright day you just might find that the color of the surface of the water is almost the same color as whatever is just above it. You may also notice that the reflection is almost a mirror image of the objects just above the water. If a breeze is blowing, there may be some curves and ripples in the reflection.

Can you see how I used one-point perspective in this drawing?

Take some time to imagine what the world would be like if kids were in charge of everything. How would things be different if the things that mattered to kids were the most important? Would the world be more fun? More fair? More beautiful? I bet there would definitely be more time for art.

News Flash!

Kids discover secret to world peace: send grumpy adults out to play.

Appendix

From Abstract Magic on page 18

You drew a face without even knowing it

From Shapes All Around You on page 24

How many triangles did you find?

From Find the Vanishing Point on page 61

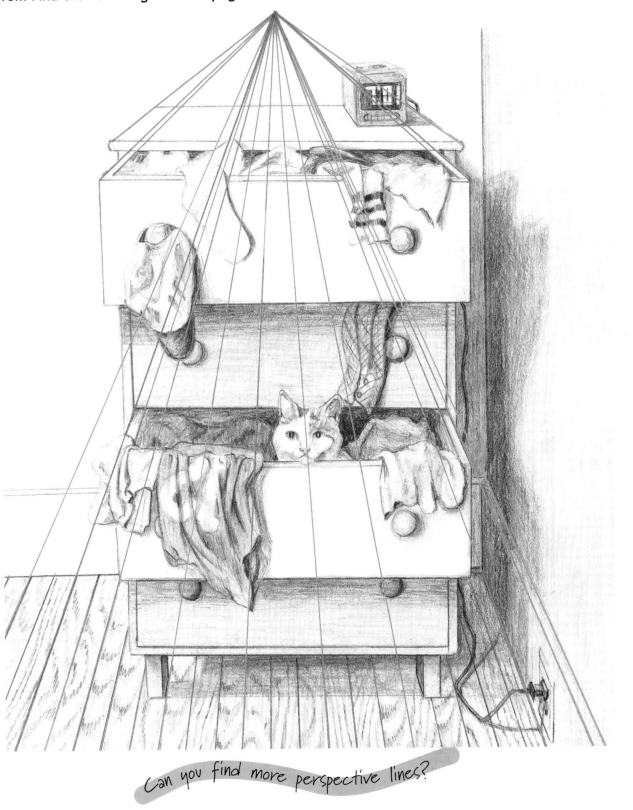

Can you find more perspective lines?

Acknowledgments

Thanks to everyone who made this book possible:

Joe Rhatigan, editor/comedian for keeping things playful, "spreading the peanut butter," trusting my creative instincts, and believing in this book; **Celia Naranjo** for her careful eye, invaluable artistic feedback, and brilliant design work; **Betty Edwards** and **Mona Brookes** for their inspiring work; **Rain Newcomb**, my friend who doubled as a colleague, for believing in me creatively and bringing me on board; **Sylvia Boyd** for teaching me to paint and showing me how to grow old; **Lizzy** and **Bruce** for cheering me on and for producing **Will**, an adorable toddler to draw and to play with, and **Claire**, whom I look forward to meeting; **Beth Trigg** for her enthusiastic affirmation and for feeding me when I was too stressed out to cook; **Mouse** the Cat (who can't even read this) for staying moderately still as I drew her and for keeping my lap warm as I wrote; **Sadie** the Dog (who also can't read) for insisting I go outside at least twice a day even when I was working around the clock on this book; **Lyme Kedic** for her patient support, faith that I had this book in me even when I doubted I did, and for playing the musical soundtrack as I drew late into the night; and **Barcley, Bailey, Lauren, Nick,** and **Geoffrey** for modeling for us.

And I couldn't possibly thank enough: **Mom** and **Dad**, for their devoted support, their creative example, and for turning off the TV when I was little.

Index